# UNIVERSITY OF CALIFORNIA LOS ANGELES

JOSH ANDERSON

childsworld.com

**Published by The Child's World®**
800-599-READ • www.childsworld.com

**Copyright © 2024 by The Child's World®**
All rights reserved. No part of this book may be reproduced or utilized in any form or by any means without written permission from the publisher.

**Photography Credits**
page 1: ©Jayne Kamin-Oncea/Stringer/Getty Images; page 2: ©Ronald Martinez/Staff/Getty Images; page 5: ©Bettmann/Contributor/Getty Images; page 7: ©J.D. Cuban/Staff/Getty Images; page 8: ©kyolshin/Getty Images; page 9: ©Brett Wilhelm/Contributor/Getty Images; page 11: ©Icon Sportswire/Contributor/Getty Images; page 12: ©Icon Sportswire/Contributor/Getty Images; page 15: ©Bettmann/Contributor/Getty Images; page 16: ©Stephen Dunn/Staff/Getty Images; page 17: ©Focus On Sport/Contributor / Getty Images; page 18: ©Bettmann/Contributor/Getty Images; page 21: ©Bettmann/Contributor/Getty Images; page 23: ©Bettmann/Contributor/Getty Images; page 24: ©Bettmann/Contributor/Getty Images; page 27: ©Michael Owens/Stringer/Getty Images; page 28: ©Grant Halverson/Contributor/Getty Images; page 29: ©Sean Gardner/Stringer/Getty Images

**ISBN Information**
9781503885202 (Reinforced Library Binding)
9781503885486 (Portable Document Format)
9781503886124 (Online Multi-user eBook)
9781503886766 (Electronic Publication)

**LCCN** 2023937560

**Printed in the United States of America**

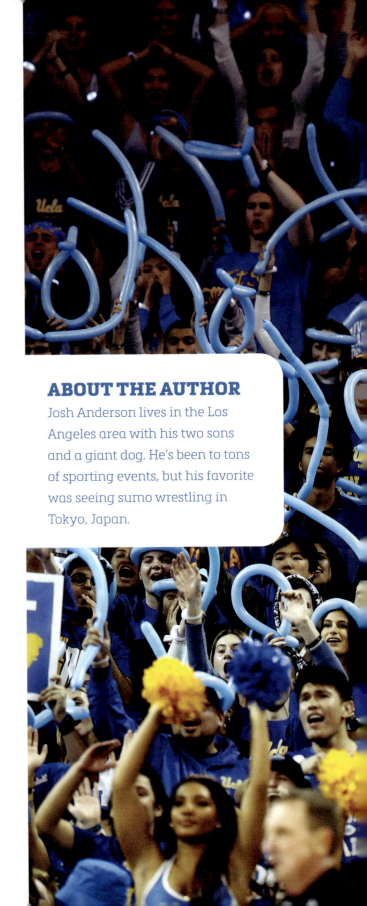

## ABOUT THE AUTHOR
Josh Anderson lives in the Los Angeles area with his two sons and a giant dog. He's been to tons of sporting events, but his favorite was seeing sumo wrestling in Tokyo, Japan.

# CONTENTS

CHAPTER ONE
## Origins . . . 4

CHAPTER TWO
## Rivalries . . . 10

CHAPTER THREE
## Great Moments . . . 14

CHAPTER FOUR
## All-Time Greats . . . 20

CHAPTER FIVE
## The Modern Era . . . 26

Glossary . . . 30

Fun Facts . . . 31

One Stride Further . . . 31

Find Out More . . . 32

Index . . . 32

CHAPTER ONE

# Origins

The University of California at Los Angeles (UCLA) opened as a teacher's college in 1882. It was called the California State Normal School at the time. The school became a part of the University of California in 1919. UCLA opened its current location in Westwood, a section of Los Angeles, in 1929. The school's first graduating class in 1925 totaled 124 people. Today, more than 47,000 students attend UCLA.

Men's basketball began at UCLA in 1919. The team's first game was against Manual Arts High School. UCLA won 46–38. The school's teams were originally called the Cubs, but they became known as the Bruins in 1926. The Bruins joined the Pacific Coast **Conference** (PCC) that same year. The PCC changed names several times and is now called the Pacific-12 (Pac-12) Conference. The UCLA men's team is the most successful one in the history of college basketball. They have won 11 **NCAA** national titles, including 7 in a row from 1967 to 1973.

The Bruins battle City College of New York in a 1949 game.

Women's basketball started at UCLA in 1974. During this time, UCLA was a part of the Association for Intercollegiate Athletics for Women (AIAW). The NCAA women's tournament did not yet exist, so the AIAW held a national basketball tournament from 1972 to 1982. The UCLA women's team won the AIAW Tournament in 1978. In 1985, the UCLA women's team joined what is now the Pac-12. The team still plays in the Pac-12 today.

## University of California, Los Angeles Bruins

**TEAM NAME:** UCLA Bruins

**FIRST SEASON:** 1919–20 (Men's Team); 1974–75 (Women's Team)

**CONFERENCE:** Pacific-12 Conference (Pac-12)

**CONFERENCE CHAMPIONSHIPS:** 32 (Men's Team); 1 (Women's Team)

**HOME ARENA:** Pauley Pavilion

**NCAA TOURNAMENT APPEARANCES:** 52 (Men's Team); 18 (Women's Team)

**NATIONAL CHAMPIONSHIPS:** 11 (Men's Team); 1 (Women's Team)

**UCLA's Amy Jalewalia (left) dribbles past a defender during a game in 1993.** ▶

## ORIGIN OF TEAM NAME

There is a bear in the center of the California state flag. Because of that, many California teams have bear-themed nicknames. UCLA was originally called the Cubs, while the University of California at Berkeley's teams were called both the Bears and the Bruins. Students at UCLA wanted a name fiercer than Cubs and adopted Grizzlies for a short time during the 1920s. But when the school joined the PCC, it couldn't have the same name as the University of Montana's teams, which were also called Grizzlies. Berkeley decided to give up the name Bruins, and UCLA adopted the name.

The first women's **All-American** at the school was Ann Meyers. Meyers was chosen as an All-American each year from 1975 to 1978. She helped lead the women to the AIAW Championship in 1978. The first men's All-American player at UCLA was Dick Linthicum in 1932. Linthicum was the first All-American in any sport at the school.

The UCLA women's team has played in the last six out of seven **NCAA Tournaments**. In 2018, the team made it to the **Elite Eight** in the NCAA Tournament for the first time since 1999. The UCLA men's team has played in five of the last six NCAA Tournaments. Their most recent **Final Four** appearance was in 2021. The men's team last won the NCAA Tournament in 1995.

The 2021 Bruins celebrate making their first Final Four appearance in more than 10 years.

CHAPTER TWO

# Rivalries

Rivals are teams who have a long history of playing each other for the right to claim they are the best. One of the Bruins' biggest basketball rivals is fellow Pac-12 team the University of Southern California (USC) Trojans. The schools are only about 12 miles (19.31 kilometers) apart. While the Bruins and Trojans will always enjoy the challenge of competing against their nearby rivals, UCLA has another tough Pac-12 foe.

The Arizona Wildcats are the only team that can come close to UCLA's success in basketball. UCLA and Arizona have won or shared 26 of the past 38 regular season men's Pac-12 titles. The Wildcats and Bruins men's teams first did battle in 1923. UCLA has won 64 of the 111 games between the schools.

One of the most memorable games between the teams took place in 2017. For the first time ever, both teams were **ranked** in the top five in the nation. The number-five ranked Bruins visited Arizona's McKale Center to play the fourth-ranked Wildcats.

**Future NBA player Aaron Holiday shoots a basket in a game with Arizona State in 2017.** ▶

10

**UCLA's Michaela Onyenwere goes for the basket.**

Although Arizona led 43–39 at halftime, UCLA guard Lonzo Ball scored 11 and dished out 8 **assists** to help UCLA come back and win 77–72.

In women's basketball, UCLA has beaten Arizona 64 times in 87 games. The teams played one of their most memorable games during the 2018–19 season. The UCLA women came into the game with a 10–9 record. They needed a strong finish to have a chance at playing in the NCAA Tournament.

As the clock wound down on the game, Arizona led 61–59. But with three seconds left, UCLA forward Michaela Onyenwere hit a layup to tie the game and send the teams to overtime. Onyenwere hit another basket with 16 seconds left in overtime to tie the game again. The teams then went to a second overtime tied 71–71.

In double overtime, it was Arizona's turn for a dramatic basket. The Bruins led 84–81 with about four seconds left. But UCLA guard Aari McDonald hit a three and sent the game to a third overtime. UCLA scored 14 points in the third overtime, including 5 free throws in the final 26 seconds. UCLA won the triple-overtime thriller 98–93. The victory over their rivals helped put UCLA on a winning path. They finished the season 22–13 and played into the **Sweet 16** round of the NCAA Tournament.

# UCLA *Ucla* VS.

# UNIVERSITY OF ARIZONA 𝔸

### First Meeting:
1923 (Men's Teams); 1977 (Women's Teams)

### UCLA's Record against Arizona:
64–47 (Men's); 64–24 (Women's)

CHAPTER THREE

# Great Moments

With 19 Final Fours and 11 national championships, the UCLA men's team has had many incredible moments. The most successful period in team history was from 1963–64 to 1974–75. During that time, coach John Wooden led the Bruins to 10 national championships, including 7 in a row.

The Bruins had four undefeated seasons during that time. Only three other teams in history have had one undefeated championship season. From 1966 to 1973, the Bruins had a 205–5 record.

John Wooden's last season at UCLA ended with the Bruins winning the 1975 NCAA Tournament. They did not win another title for nearly 20 years. Finally, during the 1994–95 season, the Bruins finished with an overall record of 31–2 and won the national championship. They were as strong as ever in the NCAA Tournament, winning their six games by an average of more than 14 points. But the Bruins almost got eliminated from the tournament in the second round.

UCLA's men's team celebrated its seventh national title in a row in 1973.

**Tyus Edney's incredible sprint down the court during the 1995 NCAA Tournament will live in the minds of Bruins fans forever.**

With UCLA ahead 73–72 in their second-round game against the Missouri Tigers, Missouri held the ball for nearly 30 seconds looking for a perfect shot. With time running out, Missouri guard Kendrick Moore scored on a layup to put the Tigers up 74–73. The Bruins had only 4.8 seconds to go the full length of the court and score.

Point guard Tyus Edney received the ball. He sped down the court, dribbled behind his back to get past a defender, and headed to the basket. Edney leapt into the air with less than a second on the clock. His layup glanced off the glass and into the hoop. UCLA had survived their one and only scare of the tournament. Two weeks later, they were crowned national champions.

The UCLA men's team hasn't won a national title since 1995. They have been to the Final Four twice since then. In 2021, after a very ordinary regular season and a fourth-place finish in the Pac-12, the Bruins made an incredible run to the Final Four that ended with a loss to top-ranked Gonzaga.

The UCLA women's team has made it to the Elite Eight round of the NCAA Tournament twice, but never further. In 2018, the Bruins defeated Texas in the Sweet 16 with 22 points and 8 assists from guard Jordin Canada.

## THAT'S STRANGE!

During the UCLA men's team's period of success in the 1960s and 1970s, the Bruins were unbeatable—almost. During the 1970–71 season, UCLA lost only one game. It was on January 23, 1971, when the Bruins visited Notre Dame University and lost 89–82. UCLA did not lose again for the rest of the 1970–71 season, and then went undefeated in 1971–72 and 1972–73. Almost exactly three years after their last loss, UCLA visited Notre Dame again. The Bruins led by 11 points with just over three minutes left. Notre Dame came back to win the game 71–70. The Bruins' record 88-game win streak had ended with a loss to the last team that had defeated them.

Ann Meyers (left) led the UCLA women's team to the national title in 1978.

The UCLA women's team's greatest moment came before the NCAA Tournament existed. In 1977–78, coach Billie Moore led the Bruins to a 27–3 record during her first season with the team. They reached the finals of the AIAW National Large College Basketball Tournament. Their opponent was the University of Maryland Terrapins. Maryland had defeated UCLA earlier that season.

But UCLA had the best player in women's college basketball. Senior forward Ann Meyers scored 20 points, had 10 rebounds, dished out 9 assists, and had 8 steals against Maryland. The Bruins won 90–74 to earn the UCLA women's only national title.

CHAPTER FOUR

# All-Time Greats

Ann Meyers played for the UCLA women's team from 1974 to 1978. Many view her as the best women's basketball player of all time. Meyers was the first woman to receive a four-year athletic scholarship from UCLA. She led UCLA to the 1978 AIAW National Championship. She finished a 1978 game with 20 points, 14 rebounds, 10 assists, and 10 steals. That made her the first player, male or female, in NCAA history to record a **quadruple-double** in a game. Meyers is also the first four-time All-American women's basketball player. In 1979, Meyers became the first woman to sign a contract with an NBA team. Although Meyers never played in an NBA game, her $50,000 contract with the Indiana Pacers was historic.

Meyers's teammate Denise Curry is the Bruins' all-time leader with 3,198 points and 1,310 rebounds. She played at UCLA from 1978 to 1981. Curry also led Team USA to a gold medal at the 1984 Olympic Games in Los Angeles.

**UCLA legend Ann Meyers holds up an Indiana Pacers jersey after signing a contract with the team.**

## THE G.O.A.T.

Lew Alcindor, later known as Kareem Abdul-Jabbar, is the greatest player in the history of UCLA men's basketball. He ranks second in points with 2,325, and rebounds with 1,367. The feat is even more amazing because Abdul-Jabbar only played three years at UCLA. He won the Associated Press Player of the Year award twice and the Naismith Award once, in the first year it was awarded. During Abdul-Jabbar's time at UCLA, the Bruins won three national titles and had a combined record of 88–2.

Billie Moore joined UCLA as the head coach of its women's team in 1977. She had led the Cal State Fullerton Titans to the 1970 National Title. When she guided the Bruins to the national championship in 1978, she became the first women's coach to lead two schools to national titles.

John Wooden was nicknamed the "Wizard of Westwood." He coached the UCLA men's team for 27 years. During that time, the team won 10 national championships. No other college coach has won more titles. Wooden was recognized as the National Coach of the Year seven times. An award for the best men's and women's players in college basketball is named for him.

**Kareem Abdul-Jabbar dunks in a game against Georgia Tech.** ▶

Center Bill Walton helped lead two of Wooden's teams to the national title. Walton is the leading rebounder in UCLA history with a total of 1,370. Walton won the Naismith Award as National Player of the Year all three years he played at UCLA. He's one of only two players to win the award three times. Walton set a record when he scored 44 points in the 1973 NCAA title game against Memphis State.

Forward Don MacLean is UCLA's all-time leading scorer. His 2,608 points are also the most in the history of the Pac-12 Conference. MacLean was a member of the All-Pac-10 Team three times during his career at UCLA.

**Bill Walton goes for a block against Indiana.**

CHAPTER FIVE

# The Modern Era

Coach Mick Cronin became head coach of the UCLA men's team in 2019–20. He led the Bruins to the NCAA Tournament three years in a row from 2021 to 2023. In 2021, UCLA reached the Final Four. The 2022–23 season was a great success for the program. The team finished with a 31–6 record and won the Pac-12 regular season title. The season ended with a loss in a thrilling game against the Gonzaga Bulldogs in the Sweet 16 of the NCAA Tournament. UCLA led by 13 points at the half, but Gonzaga roared back and won the game 79–76. After the 2022–23 season, top scorers Jaime Jaquez and Tyger Campbell graduated. Jaquez was the 2022–23 Pac-12 Player of the Year, so Cronin will have to look to his younger players for leadership in future seasons.

Coach Cori Close took over the UCLA women's program in 2011–12. She has led the Bruins to the NCAA Tournament seven times. Under Close, UCLA has advanced to the Sweet 16 five times. Their most recent trip to the Sweet 16 was in

Bruins Jaime Jaquez Jr. (left) and Johnny Juzang (right) celebrate on the court.

2023. After finishing fourth in the Pac-12, UCLA won their first-round game with Sacramento State 67–45 and their second-round contest with Oklahoma 82–73. Although the Bruins lost 59–43 to South Carolina in the Sweet 16, the team finished the season on the right path for success.

Experienced talent and new players on the UCLA roster give fans hope for more great seasons to come. With a passionate fan base and a tradition of excellence, both the men's and women's programs at UCLA have bright futures ahead.

## TEARING UP THE LEAGUE!

Jrue Holiday only played one season at UCLA, averaging 8.5 points and 3.7 assists in 2008–09. But in 14 seasons in the NBA, Holiday has become one of the top point guards in the league. Holiday has been an all-star twice and helped lead the Milwaukee Bucks to the 2021 NBA title. Holiday has also been named to an NBA All-Defensive team four times. For his career, he's averaged 16.4 points, 4.1 rebounds, and 6.5 assists per game.

◀ Gina Conti (left) attempts a layup in a 2023 NCAA Tournament game.

# GLOSSARY

**All-American (ALL uh-MAYR-uh-kin)** an athlete picked as one of the best amateurs in the United States

**assists (uh-SIST)** passes that lead directly to a basket

**conference (KON-fuhr-enss)** a group of teams that compete and play against each other every season

**Elite Eight (uh-LEET AYT)** games between the top eight teams in the NCAA Tournament

**Final Four (FY-null FOR)** games between the top four teams in the NCAA Tournament

**NCAA (National Collegiate Athletic Association)**: a group that oversees college sports in the United States

**NCAA Tournament (TUR-nuh-mint)** a competition between 68 teams at the end of the college basketball season that decides the national champion.

**quadruple-double (kwa-DROO-pull DUH-bull)** a game in which a player accumulates 10 or more in four statistical categories (example: points, rebounds, steals, and assists)

**ranked (RAYNKT)** placed on a list of individuals or teams that have accomplished high statistics in sports

**Sweet 16 (SWEET six-TEEN)** games between the top 16 teams in the NCAA Tournament

## FUN FACTS

- All-time leading scorer Denise Curry set the record for most points scored in a game by a member of the Bruins women's team. She scored 47 in a 1979 game against Oregon State.

- Lew Alcindor (Kareem Abdul-Jabbar) has the four highest-scoring games in UCLA men's history. He set the school record in a 1967 game against Washington State when he scored 61 points.

- Three UCLA women have grabbed 25 rebounds in a game. The most recent was Monique Billings in 2017.

- Jelani McCoy is the all-time leader in blocked shots for the UCLA men's team with 188.

- The UCLA women's team has dominated the Washington State Cougars, winning 60 of their 72 matchups.

## ONE STRIDE FURTHER

- Coach John Wooden gets a lot of credit from fans for UCLA's incredible success on the court in the 1960s and 1970s. Who do you think is most responsible for a team's success, its coach or its players? Come up with three reasons to support your point of view and write them down. Then, ask your friends and family what they think.

- Make a list of your favorite college basketball players. Include two things about each player that make them your favorite. Is it the way they play? Their attitude on the court? What else?

- Ask your friends and family members about their favorite sport. Keep track and make a graph to see which sport wins out.

# FIND OUT MORE

## IN THE LIBRARY

Berglund, Bruce. *Basketball GOATs: The Greatest Athletes of All Time.* New York, NY: Sports Illustrated Kids, 2022.

Buckley, Jr., James. *It's a Numbers Game! Basketball.* Washington, DC: National Geographic Kids, 2020.

Editors of *Sports Illustrated for Kids. My First Book of Basketball.* New York, NY: Sports Illustrated Kids, 2023.

Williamson, Ryan. *College Basketball Hot Streaks.* Parker, CO: The Child's World, 2020.

## ON THE WEB

Visit our website for links about UCLA basketball:

**childsworld.com/links**

*Note to Parents, Caregivers, Teachers, and Librarians: We routinely verify our web links to make sure they are safe and active sites. So encourage your readers to check them out!*

Abdul-Jabbar, Kareem 22
Arizona Wildcats 10

Ball, Lonzo 12

Campbell, Tyger 26
Canada, Jordin 17
Close, Cori 26
Cronin, Mick 26
Curry, Denise 20

Edney, Tyus 17

Jaquez, Jaime 26–7

Linthicum, Dick 8

MacLean, Don 25
McDonald, Aari 13
Meyers, Ann 8, 18–20
Moore, Billie 16, 19, 22

Onyenwere, Michaela 12–13

Pac-12 Conference 4, 6, 10, 17, 25–26, 29

Walton, Bill 25
Wooden, John 14, 22, 25

32